DATE DUE

D1361766

THE HISTORY OF PUNISHMENT

Crime and Detection series

- Criminal Terminology
- Cyber Crime
- Daily Prison Life
- Death Row and Capital Punishment
- Domestic Crime
- Famous Prisons
- Famous Trials
- Forensic Science
- Government Intelligence Agencies
- Hate Crimes
- The History and Methods of Torture
- The History of Punishment
- International Terrorism
- Major Unsolved Crimes
- Organized Crime
- Protecting Yourself Against Criminals
- Race and Crime
- Serial Murders
- The United States Justice System
- The War Against Drugs

CRIME AND DETECTION

THE HISTORY OF PUNISHMENT

MICHAEL KERRIGAN

MASON CREST PUBLISHERS
www.masoncrest.com

Mason Crest Publishers, Inc.
370 Reed Road
Broomall, PA 19008
(866) MCP-BOOK (toll free)
www.masoncrest.com

13 12 11 10 09 08 07 06 05   10 9 8 7 6 5 4 3 2

Library of Congress Cataloging-in-Publication Data

Kerrigan, Michael.
  The history of punishment / Michael Kerrigan.
        v. cm.—(Crime and detection)
  Includes bibliographical references and index.
  Contents: Introduction—The wages of sin—A debt to society—Corporal punishment—Capital
  punishment—The rise of rehabilitation.
  ISBN 1-59084-386-X
  1. Punishment—History—Juvenile literature. [1. Punishment.] I. Title. II. Series.
  HV8501.K48 2003

     364.6—dc21

                                      2003000

Editorial and design by
Amber Books Ltd.
Bradley's Close
47–77 White Lion Street
London N1 9PF
www.amberbooks.co.uk

Project Editor: Michael Spilling
Design: Floyd Sayers
Picture Research: Natasha Jones

Printed and bound in Malaysia

Picture credits
AKG London: 40–41, 61; Corbis: 44, 45, 53, 74, 79; Mary Evans Picture Library: 14, 16,
22–23, 27, 30, 32, 35, 36, 46, 48–49, 51, 57; Popperfoto: 29, 42, 67, 69, 89; Topham
Picturepoint: 6, 8, 10, 11, 13, 15, 17, 21, 25, 26, 33, 39, 50, 52, 54, 55, 58, 60, 63, 64, 65, 66,
71, 72, 75, 76, 77, 80, 81, 83, 84, 85, 87.
Front Cover: Topham Picturepoint (top left), Corbis (top right), Topham Picturepoint (bottom).

CONTENTS

Introduction

From the moment in the Book of Genesis when Cain's envy of his brother Abel erupted into violence, crime has been an inescapable feature of human life. Every society ever known has had its own sense of how things ought to be, its deeply held views on how men and women should behave. Yet in every age there have been individuals ready to break these rules for their own advantage: they must be resisted if the community is to thrive.

This exciting and vividly illustrated series of books sets out the history of crime and detection from the earliest times to the present day, from the empires of the ancient world to the towns and cities of the 21st century. From the commandments of the great religions to the theories of modern psychologists, it considers changing attitudes toward offenders and their actions. Contemporary crime is examined in its many different forms: everything from racial hatred to industrial espionage, from serial murder to drug trafficking, from international terrorism to domestic violence.

The series looks, too, at the heroic work of those men and women entrusted with the task of overseeing and maintaining law and order, from judges and court officials to police officers and other law enforcement agents. The tools and techniques at their disposal are described in detail, and the ethical issues they face are concisely and clearly explained.

All in all, the *Crime and Detection* series provides a comprehensive and accessible account of this exciting world, in theory and in practice, past and present.

CHARLIE FULLER

Executive Director, International Association of Undercover Officers

Left: An Afghan fighter stands defiant before a British firing squad during the Afghan War of 1878-80—a terrorist in their eyes, but no doubt an idealist in his own. The firing squad has always been the prefered method of execution for the military.

The Wages of Sin

Some sense of order has underpinned every human society in history, as much in "savage" tribes as in "advanced" civilizations. The recognition that the impulses of the individual have to be held in restraint for the good of the wider group is central to every culture ever known. This tendency is so universal, in fact, that one might assume it was deeply rooted in our nature; yet in some ways, it would appear that the opposite is the case. Our instinct is generally to put our individual wants first: social order has had to be redefined and reasserted in every generation. However, it is our duty as a society to order ourselves as scrupulously as we can: that we cannot judge infallibly should not prevent our even trying.

Community spirit has never been something a civilized society could take for granted; its requirements have always been expressed explicitly in laws and enforced by authority. Even then, our idea of what might or might not be permissible has not been strong enough in itself to ensure our conformity: society's rules are backed up by the fear of punishment. From the spontaneous parental slap to the solemn ceremony of the state execution, from amputations to parking fines, punishment has existed in almost every day and age as the means by which society has sought to keep its own wayward members under collective control.

Nice as it might be to do without it, punishment is a necessary evil that has enabled society to realize its "better self." Like all things human, it is

Left: Here, people attempt to gain entrance to heaven; many are rejected, and are pulled down towards hell. Taken from a 12th century Byzantine icon, this painting demonstrates the medieval Christian belief in divine punishment. The threat of hell was used by the clergy and authorities as the ultimate sanction to deter sinful actions.

Throughout history, it has been felt that justice should not just be done, but should be *seen* to be done for the benefit of society. The stocks of medieval Europe took this idea to extremes, being basically a way of exhibiting offenders.

flawed: states, like parents, may make mistakes, and the punishments of one society are often regarded with disapproval—even outright horror—by another.

STONE-AGE SCRUPLES

There *was* once a golden age: the earliest-known human societies appear to have gotten along quite well without any need of laws or punishment at all. "Hunter-gatherer" groups, they lived nomadically—moving from place to

The life of the Kalahari !Kung has strong religious and ethical dimensions, yet the very simplicity of their circumstances has made unnecessary the need for any explicit code of what we would call law.

place across vast territories—hunting wild animals for meat and gathering fruit, roots, and other plant foods. Their lives certainly included a religious dimension, with offerings to **totemic** beasts and ancestral spirits, but the rules of social behavior would have been accepted without question by all members of the group.

Studies of surviving communities of this kind, such as the Amazon Indians or !Kung Bushmen of southern Africa's Kalahari Desert, suggest a lifestyle based on sharing and cooperation. Authority in the tribal group is shared equally according to a system of what anthropologists call "dispersed leadership."

Given their nomadic lifestyle, hunter-gatherers have always traveled extremely light, with few possessions, and consequently little motive for theft or even **covetousness**. Thrown together as closely as they are by the difficulties of getting by in the wilderness, such communities live right on top of one another. They often regulate themselves without even noticing, having no physical place for concealment, nor even the mental space for anything much in the way of private thoughts.

We should recall this whenever we find ourselves making contemptuous use of the word "primitive." Peoples who pursue such stone-age lifestyles may know nothing of cars or computers, but they know nothing of crime or greed either.

All that changed for our distant ancestors with the "Neolithic revolution," when the domestication of certain animal and plant species encouraged communities to settle down in one place as the first farmers. This enabled the systematic accumulation of "riches" in the form of surplus resources, the beginning of differences in wealth and influence. Many evils stemmed from this, from envy and exploitation to robbery and murder. One of the most curious ironies of human history is that we seem to have been at our most "civilized" (in the sense of being humane and generous) in our most "savage" state. It was only when we started building larger communities and states, with such trappings of "civilization" as art and

Ox-horned Hathor, goddess of the sky, and the hawk-headed Horus, protector of the pharaoh, both owed homage to the great Osiris, ancient Egyptian god of judgment and the underworld.

learning and more elaborate religious **creeds**, that we began to reveal our more aggressive, unpleasant side. Hence, the need for bodies of law to keep societies in line and the need to back these laws up with a variety of punishments.

A LIFE HEREAFTER

All religious systems resemble one another in that they all have their own sense of **ethics**—of "right" and "wrong"—however different their values may have been in their particular details. Among the many other things Christianity took from Judaism was a belief in the eternal life of the individual, although different Christian churches (like different wings of Judaism) disagreed over whether the physical body, or just the soul or spirit, would be resurrected. Most creeds known to us today have held that transgressions committed in the course of this life will have their

LIFE AFTER LIFE AFTER LIFE

Divine judgment is even more central to the beliefs of Buddhism, an Eastern religion of Indian origin in which the individual soul is held to have many afterlives. The life any creature is currently living, say Buddhists, is only one phase in the endless cycle of death and rebirth known as *samsara*: when it ends, its existence will simply be renewed in another form.

The principle of *karma* (the belief that every action will have its consequences in this or in a later life) governs the progress of the soul up and down through the various states of existence. Depending on how well the creature has lived, it may be reborn in a higher or lower form. From the lowest bug to the highest bodhisattva (holy man), every living thing has an equal claim to eternal life. The human phase is special, because only in this form can the individual embrace Buddhism and achieve the sacred level of *nirvana*, in which the soul escapes the ceaseless swirl of *samsara* to attain a final state of utter calm. The same idea of ceaseless death and rebirth exists in slightly different versions in other Indian religions, especially Hinduism and Jainism.

punishment in another existence to come—that God (or the gods) will sit in judgment on every individual.

There have been exceptions, of course—notably the view of the classical Greeks that the afterlife was for all, regardless of rank or conduct, an awful eternity of dark and dreariness. For the ancient Egyptians, on the other hand, the afterlife to come was strikingly similar to that lived by mortals on earth. Their god, Osiris, set the souls of the dead to work in his fields and storehouses to earn their "keep," just as ordinary Egyptians had to work for

The jaws of hell gape wide for the souls of sinners in this illumination from a medieval Christian manuscript: the monks who illustrated such manuscripts seem to have taken a perverse pleasure in imagining the torments of the damned.

Escorted by the Archangel Gabriel, Muhammad ascends triumphantly to heaven in this painting from a 15th-century Persian manuscript. Though so long locked in rivalry with the countries of the West, Islam shares much, theologically, with both Christianity and Judaism.

This illustration from the 14th-century Holkham Bible shows the Last Judgement. The fear of ultimate judgement before God has always been a cornerstone of Christian ethics, and one that attempts to make people take responsibility for their actions, good or bad.

the pharaoh in their time on earth. The individual's social status in the afterlife, and the sort of labors he or she would be expected to perform, would have depended in part on the **piety** he or she had previously shown.

DEATH AND JUDGMENT, HEAVEN AND HELL

The earliest Jewish writings are silent on the nature of the afterlife. However, beginning in 500 B.C., the idea that the individual's existence endured beyond the moment of death gradually gained ground. Orthodox Jews came to believe that the body, however badly disintegrated or decayed, would be brought together at the end of the world and allocated its place in either eternal blessing or everlasting torment.

Christianity took much of its doctrine from the traditions of Judaism, and its approach to "eschatology" (the theology of the "four last things": death, judgment, heaven, and hell) was no exception. Increasingly, in modern times, liberal Christians (like liberal Jews) have discarded the idea of bodily resurrection, seeing immortality as confined to the individual's essential spirit or soul. The same basic principle applies, however: for the virtuous individual, perfect happiness awaits, while an eternity of suffering awaits the sinner.

Islam is known as the third of the "religions of the book," since, like Christianity, it is based on a belief in the Old Testament of the Bible. It is hardly surprising, therefore, that its idea of the afterlife should resemble theirs. However, the Arabs added their own distinctive emphasis to the established image: the desert-dwelling Prophet Muhammad envisioned a paradise that clearly resembled an oasis—a green garden sanctuary through whose grounds crystal fountains flow, beside which beauteous maidens will tend to each individual.

Exactly how literally the devout Muslim should expect such rewards to be realized in paradise is not clear. Under Islam, as under Judaism and Christianity, controversy has raged down the generations over how far scriptural accounts of heaven and hell should be seen as descriptions of

WHOSE VENGEANCE?

By what right—or duty—do we exact punishment from those considered to have committed crimes? The dispute between what we would now call "conservatives" and "liberals" is nearly as old as the Judeo-Christian tradition. The place of retribution in scripture is clear: "Vengeance is mine; I will repay, saith the Lord," writes St. Paul in his Epistle to the Romans (12, 19), echoing the words of Deuteronomy, 32, 35.

However, upon reading the words closely (and down the centuries, rival groups of scholars have read them very closely indeed), they appear to be open to two completely opposite interpretations. One interpretation—the more conservative—suggests that the verse ties the ideas of divinity and punishment inextricably together: "I bring vengeance, says God: that is what I do"—and so, by implication, it is what you should do, too.

The liberal interpretation reads the verse as meaning "Vengeance is mine—meaning, not yours": humans should not think of judging—still less of inflicting punishment—for themselves. While few would seriously argue that mortal men and women have no business making laws or administering punishment at all, there remains a sincere and strongly felt division between the hard-liners and the liberals where law and order are concerned.

actual places, and how far they should be seen as symbolic representations of spiritual fulfillment on the one hand or desolation on the other.

In the Western tradition, then, the afterlife can be seen as a divine reflection of the earthly existence in which the individual, judged by God, is punished or rewarded. At the same time, however, believers felt it their duty to attempt to realize God's kingdom on earth, which meant incorporating divine law into everyday routine.

DIRECT INTERVENTION FROM GOD

Moses' descent from the slopes of Mount Sinai with the Ten Commandments inscribed on tablets is only the most famous of several direct interventions by which the God of the Bible attempted to govern the lives of men and women. Moses was believed to have drawn up an entire system of law, the Halakhah, for his people. This would form the basis of the Talmud, that codification in which the essentials of the Torah, the teachings of Judaism, are set down.

There is more to the Talmud than law: everything from folklore to proverbial wisdom is included. However, the Jews were preeminent among early peoples in their attempts to prescribe the rules of good spiritual and social conduct. Their beliefs did much to form our own modern notions of crime and punishment. Previous civilizations may have had extensive lists of religious prohibitions on specific activities, foods, and drinks (rather as the Jews themselves did in the Book of Leviticus), but what we would see as the individual's moral duty to those around him or her evolved only slowly over thousands of years.

The duty to reject a certain type of food is essentially an arbitrary restriction, established simply to test the loyalty and obedience of the individual believer. The commandments against covetousness or murder, on the other hand, clearly involved a sense of the rights of other people. Many modern scholars argue that the development of this sensibility was the great achievement of the Jews, although at this historical distance, it is impossible to make the claim with any real certainty.

Whoever has the honor of having made the moral and philosophical breakthrough involved, the realization that the individual should respect the rights of his or her neighbors was clearly a key moment in the history of what we would think of as "civilization." We should not exaggerate its

In this magnificent painting by the 17th-century Dutch artist Rembrandt van Rijn, Moses descends from Sinai, bearing the tablets of the Jewish Law. The grandeur of Van Rijn's work makes clear his sense of the momentousness of an episode in which an entire tradition of moral values started.

impact, however, because long before men and women had consciously articulated these concerns, they were present in the ritual and religious background.

SOCIAL RULES PROMOTED ON RELIGIOUS GROUNDS

What were once regarded as ritual recommendations were often aimed at the protection of society. The incest taboo is a case in point: had it not been for the powerful religious prohibition on sexual relationships within families, such

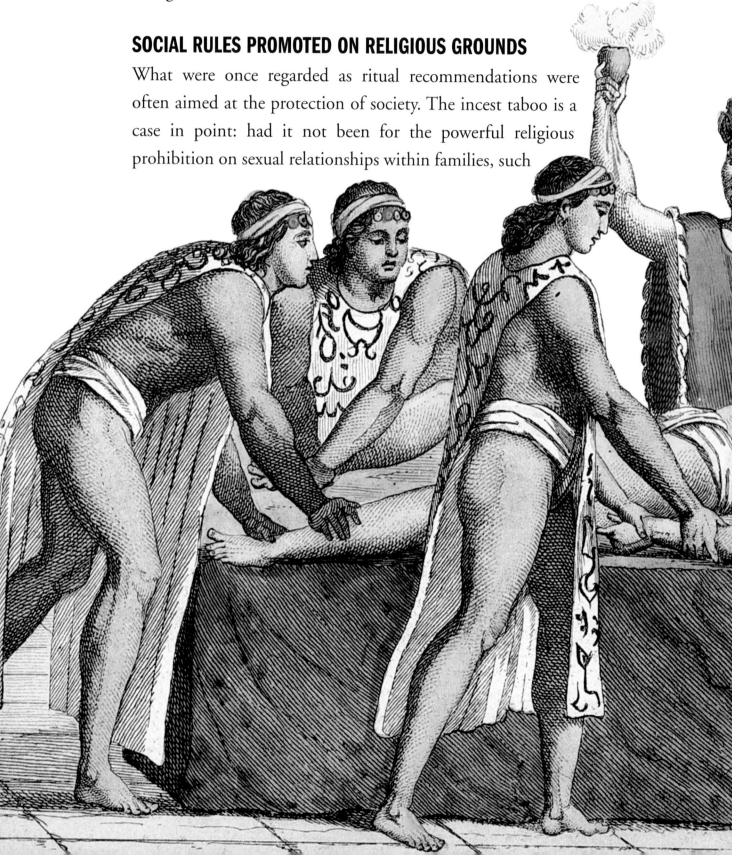

contact might have seemed an obvious way for small and far-flung communities to perpetuate themselves. The fearful genetic consequences of this sort of in-breeding would have become clear only over time: the religious ban thus serves a practical social purpose.

The original inhabitants of the Americas seem, like the early civilizations of the Old World, to have exacted punishments both for ritual transgressions and for what we might see as socially defined crimes. If you conspired against the authority of the Sapa Inca, the ruler of the Inca empire of the ancient Andes, you could expect to be hurled into a dungeon stocked with snakes and other fearsome creatures. Adultery across the boundaries of rank was also seen as a sacrilege punishable by death. Here, again, we see the fierce enforcement of social rules justified on religious grounds: without respect for the established hierarchy, Inca society would have been destabilized.

The Aztecs of Mexico also maintained social stability by means of a system of taboos. Each class had its appointed style of dress and personal presentation. To wear the wrong hairstyle or clothing was a crime punishable by death: cotton, for

An Aztec priest at Tenochtitlan, Mexico, tears the heart from a still-living victim—yet such sacrifices had nothing to do with punishment as we understand it.

example, was a right of the nobility. Other laws covered exploitative commercial practices: fraud and theft were severely punished, as was corruption on the part of judges and officials. Despite the fact that—to our modern minds—their down-to-earth practicality is plain, these laws were seen as religiously ordained.

Yet even more seemingly pointless prohibitions may have a role beyond the ritual in helping to reinforce an individual's identity. Think, for example, of the dietary tightrope the Orthodox Jew must walk each day to keep **kosher** laws and shun the unfit **terefah**. These restrictions are a constant reminder to the Jew of just who he or she is, of the spiritual tradition to which Jews belong, and the religious and historical differences that separate their community from other sections of society.

UPHOLDING HINDUISM

Another example of how social laws are promoted along religious lines is found in India. According to the great Indian creed of Hinduism, the entire created universe follows certain rules; those laws that govern human life are only a part of this general order. The Sanskrit word *dharma* (from *dhar*, meaning to uphold) refers, therefore, not only to what we would see as social morality and spiritual observance, but also to what we might tend to think of as the laws of nature.

The *Manusmrti*, or "Laws of Manu"—supposedly set down at the beginning of the world by the semidivine lawmaker Manu—can be seen as a sort of Hindu Talmud. Its 12 books contain a wealth of spiritual wisdom, ceremonial instructions, and social rules. Not that the Hindu writers of the third to first centuries B.C.—who are thought to have been the code's actual authors—would have made the distinctions we do today between these different categories. The decree that this or that food is forbidden or that some action is "unclean" might seem arbitrary to us, but they can often be explained in social terms.

Today, for example, the *Manusmrti* are notorious in the West for their

The reclining figure of a Mayan god sprawls majestically among the ruins at Chichen Itza, Yucatán, Mexico. It is thought that the god's lap was used as an altar for bloody human sacrifices.

In Hinduism, as in other religions, divinity has both its benign and its more frightening aspects:
the goddess Kali is feared as a force for a vengeful and destructive justice.

Here is a frightening image of Fudo, the Japanese god of punishment. He carries a sword to smite the wicked and a rope to bind them.

formulation of India's age-old "caste system"—a scale that established the worth of particular social groups, categorizing Indians rigidly, from the patrician Brahmins to the despised "untouchables." Thus, a tradition based in religious ritual can be seen to have had a clear (if, from our point of view, disagreeable and indeed damaging) social function, establishing a hierarchy in which every Indian knew his or her place.

TABOO

Taken from the Polynesian word tapu (meaning "marked off"), a taboo was originally any action, place, person, animal, or object on which special status had been conferred by the powers of the gods. This status was by no means necessarily negative—a taboo was just as likely to be a good thing as a bad one. In modern terms, perhaps, it had as much to do with fortune as it did with morality: in some ways, its properties resembled those of a rabbit's foot or other lucky charm.

The idea that a taboo was specifically a bad, forbidden thing was the invention of 20th-century psychologists, such as Sigmund Freud. Yet if the Freudian psychologists' was so narrow an interpretation of the original meaning as to amount to a distortion, their notion was too valuable to the modern world to be dispensed with.

The term "taboo" came to be applied to those fundamentally forbidden things that are considered off-limits in any given culture. The most famous taboo—perhaps because it has been the most universal—has been the prohibition against incest. Yet most cultures have other taboos as well, whether regarding the eating of particular plants or animals or regarding a wide variety of different forbidden activities.

Hindu women pray, thronged in their thousands in the shallows of the sacred Brahmaputra River, where it flows through Bangladesh: its waters will, they believe, wash away all stains of sin.

A Debt to Society

As we have seen, laws that claim to have a religious justification often have an underlying social role, helping to ensure the orderly functioning of a community in everyday life. At first, this purpose, however important, tended to be understood and was generally unconscious; over time, however, it came increasingly into the open.

By classical times, with the establishment of the great civilizations of Greece and Rome, a **secular** concern for social order existed quite independent of religious rules, and lawmakers saw no reason to appeal to any higher thing than the public good. The legal system the Romans set in place provided the foundation for modern Western law, and has an influence to this day.

Yet the gradual separation of worldly order from the religious rules that had gone before gave rise to a new difficulty, that of coming up with an adequate punishment. An offense against an all-powerful god might result in an eternity's suffering, but why should any individual worry about incurring the wrath of society? Rulers quickly saw the need for their laws to be backed up by the threat (and the reality) of punishment if the smooth running of society was to be maintained.

THE UTILITY PRINCIPLE

Every society needs a system of laws if order and coherence are to be maintained. Simple "utility" (social practicality) would demand this, even if no god decreed it. What philosophers call "utilitarianism"—the belief that societies should strive for "the greatest happiness of the greatest

Left: Author Daniel Defoe was placed in the pillory in 1703, after one of his satires upset the English government of the day. Fortunately, a sympathetic crowd showered him with flowers and heartfelt praises, rather than with the usual rocks, dead rats, and other rubbish.

Joachin, King of Judah, is released from prison by the Babylonian evil emperor Merodach in a modern engraving of a scene said to have taken place around 587 B.C.

The labor camps of both czarist Russia and the Communist Soviet Union punished political dissent in the cruelest way: many were—quite literally—worked to death doing the hardest work under the harshest conditions.

number"—requires that individuals recognize the need for their freedom to be limited for the sake of those around them. This need exists regardless of whatever any deity may demand.

The defiantly godless Soviet Union was one of the most strictly policed societies ever seen. In fact, the confirmed **atheism** of that state was a key factor in its cruel repression of just about every impulse to freedom among its people, its Communist rulers feeling the need to play the part that, in another country, was played by the individual conscience.

Often, laws that seem to have a religious foundation have in fact been created by rulers for their own benefit. This charge has often been leveled at the first known body of written law, the Hammurabi Code of ancient Babylon (c.1700 B.C.). Scholars have pointed out how some of its 282 clauses justify seizures of land made by King Hammurabi himself, but in fairness, its statutes are extensive in their scope as these extracts illustrate: "If fire breaks out in a man's house and a man who goes to put it out helps himself to the owner's possessions, that man should be thrown into the fire. If thieves and robbers gather in a woman's wine shop and she takes no steps to alert the authorities, then that wine seller shall herself be put to death."

"THE SCIENCE OF THE JUST AND THE UNJUST"

For a system of secular law that is primarily rooted not in religious, but in social values, we have to look to the Twelve Tables (c. 450 B.C.) of ancient Rome. While some of their stipulations impress us now with their honest-to-goodness simple virtue ("a man might gather up fruit that was falling down onto another man's farm"; "let them keep the road in order; if they have not paved it, a man may drive his team where he likes"), others suggest a more sophisticated appreciation of the law. Their key contribution lay in the importance they attributed to what we would now call "due process"— the proper carrying out of legal procedures, with full protection for defendants' rights and an opportunity for both sides of a case to be heard and debated.

Furthermore, the insistence of Table IX, Clause 6, that, "The putting to death of any man, whosoever he might be, unconvicted, is forbidden," represented a revolution in social thinking, however basic it might seem today. It is hard to overestimate the significance of this shift in attitudes, just as it is hard to overestimate the Romans' reverence for their law. Previous civilizations saw their social rules as the creation of their respective deities, but for the Romans, the opposite seems to have been the case. Their goddess Iustitia, "Justice," seems to have existed mainly as a metaphor—

Here, in heroic terms, a modern engraving captures the mood of the moment around 450 B.C.
when the "Twelve Tables" were made the basis for Roman law. To us, perhaps, the law may seem
like something gray and boring, but to ancient peoples, it only too clearly made the difference
between barbaric anarchy and civilized life.

Flanked by his wife Theodora, the Emperor Justinian I is seen here holding a scroll: his codification of the law laid the foundations for the modern science of "jurisprudence."

"PUNISHMENT" AS PROPAGANDA

The ancient Assyrians were early discoverers of the idea that punishment might "send out a signal." A mighty race of warriors whose heartland was in what we now know as Iraq, the Assyrians were renowned throughout the ancient Middle East for their military skill, but were also feared for their ruthlessness.

Whenever they took an enemy city, they skinned some of their prisoners alive, hanging others from their city walls to die of thirst and heat exhaustion. That this was really a "punishment" at all is, of course, debatable—although that does seem to be the way the Assyrians saw it. By today's standards, it seems a grim penalty for the dubious "crime" of resisting an invader. The Assyrians' real—if perhaps subconscious—purpose was quite clearly to demoralize their defeated foes and warn others of the risks of holding out against them.

that is, as a personification of the spirit of the law. The legal system itself received the respect that would once have been reserved for a divinity.

THE SPREAD OF ROMAN LAW

As the centuries wore on, the Roman Empire extended its reach across the known world, imposing its government on the populations of what are now no fewer than 33 different sovereign states, from Scotland to Syria. However, the common-sense simplicities of the Twelve Tables were not adequate to so vast and complex a political construction.

The Romans did try hard to stay true to their underlying principles even as their legal system grew and grew. To a remarkable extent, they succeeded: Roman law remained admirably logical and coherent, qualities still evident in the massive codification drawn up by the Emperor Justinian in the

Empire's dying days in the sixth century A.D. By this time, the great Roman Empire was a shattered ruin, Rome itself having been abandoned to the barbarians; the imperial center had been transported eastward two centuries earlier to Byzantium (modern Istanbul).

Yet great pride was taken in what had been, and many traditions were kept alive, not the least being the Roman respect for the law. The "Justinian Code" set out to record "the science of the just and the unjust"—itself a revolution in perception, implying that the law could be understood in terms of human knowledge and logic without reference to a higher power. The many thousands of laws it covered came down to three essential truths: "to live honestly, to hurt no one, to give every one his due."

"TO GIVE EVERY ONE HIS DUE"

What we think of as "modern" Western law is in large part drawn directly from the Roman model, and these three truths underlie our own American legal system right down to the present day. Yet we—like the Romans before us—have found them far easier to aspire to than to fulfill, especially where the ideals of legal philosophy run up against the hard realities of human life. In truth, to "live honestly" as a society, we have found it necessary to "hurt" some—those guilty of offenses—precisely to ensure that we "give every one his due." In fact, punishment may serve several different social purposes—something that can make discussion of the already complex rights and wrongs even more difficult.

Seen at its simplest as a form of retribution for wrongdoing, punishment is also supposed to deter the criminal from repeating an offense. (At its most basic level, punishment may be no more than a way of physically preventing further crimes: a murderer who has been executed certainly will not be doing it again. And, whether or not you consider it an effective means of combating criminality in the longer term, imprisonment at least serves the short-term purpose of containing the criminal—behind bars, at least, the prisoner will not be re-offending.) However, punishment should

A chain gang marches out from a facility in Huntsville, Alabama: these men will spend the day working in the fields. Opinions are divided as to the effectiveness of this form of punishment, but it certainly keeps the prisoners busy and lets them give something back to the local community.

further serve as a deterrent to others in society who might be tempted into transgression and, perhaps, reassure the law-abiding citizens that their legal system is looking out for them.

SEEING JUSTICE DONE

The view that "justice must be seen to be done" runs deep in the modern Western consciousness: the feeling that criminals are getting away with something places the entire social structure under strain. Why, ask respectable citizens, should we pay our taxes, keep litter laws, or honor parking regulations when we see others committing more serious crimes with impunity?

There has always, therefore, been a distinct presentational aspect to punishment—a sense in which it is meant as much to encourage the law-abiding as to discourage the criminal. The notion of punishment-by-example was taken to extremes in the stocks of medieval Europe. For those found guilty of minor crimes, being placed in stocks was essentially a ritual of public shaming. Two heavy boards hinged together, with holes for the heads and feet, the stocks offered a form of outdoor, highly public imprisonment. A bartender who persistently watered down his drinks, a trader selling substandard goods, an incorrigible drunk: any of these might be exposed in the stocks for an afternoon to face the full force of public derision. So, too, since the typical stocks could hold two prisoners at once, might an adulterous couple or a quarrelsome man and wife.

The importance of the punishment was twofold: not only did it directly act on those sentenced to endure the ordeal, but it also gave the whole community a sense of involvement in the doing of justice. Placed prominently in every community in the main street or by the village green, the stocks stood—even when unoccupied—as a powerful symbol of the rule of law. The later **pillory** served a similar purpose, although punishment here seems to have been more unpleasant, even physical, with crowds pelting prisoners with everything from dead rats to rocks—on occasion with fatal consequences. Yet while Western societies today have rejected such punishments as fundamentally inhuman because the element of "mob law" they involve is felt to be uncivilized, we still recognize the need of the wider community to feel a sense of involvement in the legal process.

The appearance of TV cameras in our courtrooms in the last few decades has been one response to this perception: televised trials let the public see the law in action and come to a greater understanding of how it works. On

The beauty of the pillory as punishment was that it enabled the whole community to feel involved with the workings of the law–but it also enabled the venting of some extremely ugly emotions.

The workings of *sharia* can vary greatly from place to place, sometimes impressing by its humanity, at others appalling by its barbarism. This Nigerian woman (center, with child) was sentenced to death by stoning for adultery—despite her defense that this "crime" had been forced on her by rape.

the negative side, such proceedings have the potential to become a media circus—as happened when football and movie star O.J. Simpson was put on trial in the early 1990s. The fear that the media tail may wag the justice dog is redoubled when wider social issues seem to be at stake, as when the L.A. police officers accused of beating up black man Rodney King in 1991 went before the court. Their acquittal by a white jury was the signal for several days of serious rioting in South Central Los Angeles: the legal system was felt to have let the people down.

VICTIMS' JUSTICE

In recent years, many in Western society have argued that the victims of crime should have some say in—or derive some benefit from—the perpetrators' punishment. Thus, those who have suffered at the hands of violent attackers can testify to the traumas they have undergone, while young thugs are set to work on community projects in those neighborhoods they have previously terrorized.

There are parallels here with the traditions of Islamic *sharia* law—the Arabic word means, literally, "the well-worn path." Some Westerners today tend to think of Muslims as religious fanatics and to associate Islamic countries with punishments of "medieval" cruelty—execution by beheading and the amputation of limbs—yet this is an oversimplification. In fact, the Koran, the holy book in which the divinely dictated words of the Prophet Muhammad are recorded, has a strong sense of social value, and sees such punishments as a last resort. Rather, it urges victims or their families (who are given a great deal of influence over what punishment an Islamic court should exact) to accept appropriate compensation for wrongs committed. Instead of demanding the death of a murderer, then, a victim's kin should settle for a sum of money—no punishment will bring back their beloved relative, after all. And is it not far better, asks the Koran, that a thief be set to work to repay the sum that was stolen, rather than suffering mutilation or being locked away to nobody's advantage?

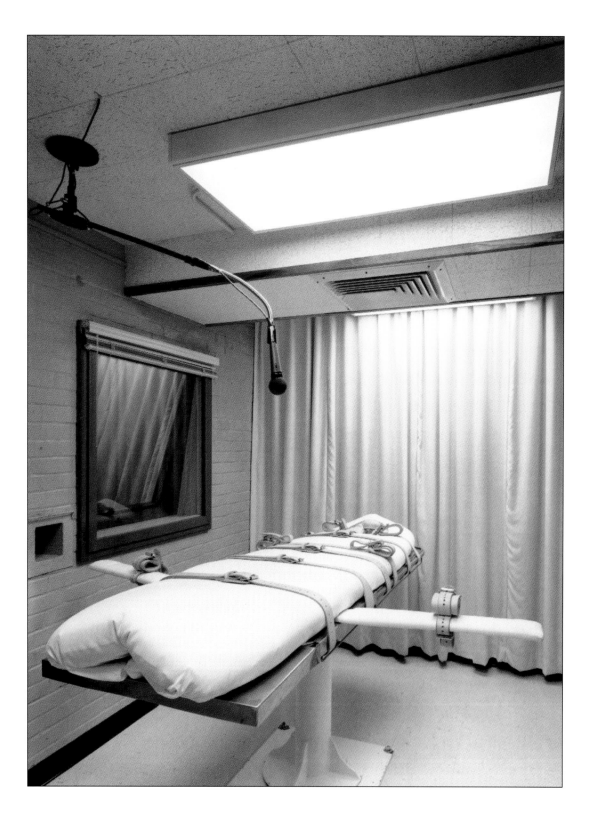

The ultimate sanction, the death penalty, is still practiced in many countries today, including the United States. Here, the couch and straps of the lethal injection chamber in Huntsville, Texas, lies ready for the next offender.

The forbidding face of the modern penal institution is seen in this view of a state prison in Pennsylvania: those who will not keep society's rules may have to be kept in a place apart to protect the general public.

Corporal Punishment

The idea that punishment should be about pain has seemed self-evident to many cultures—it has been replaced only relatively recently in our own culture. Indeed, to many people in modern America, the "mere" deprivation of liberty represented by imprisonment still seems an inadequate penalty to have to pay: the criminal should have to feel for himself some of the suffering he has caused his victims.

There can be no doubt that corporal—that is, bodily—punishment does have an immediate impact upon us: a parental smack speaks eloquently, even to the preverbal child. Precisely what it *says* is another matter. Many psychologists feel the message it sends is profoundly damaging, but all agree that physical pain is impossible to ignore.

Not that this is the only sort of distress involved: there is also the indignity, especially when the penalty is exacted—as it so often is—in front of other people. In some societies, a symbolic logic may exist between the criminal's body and the crime committed—the amputation of a thief's hand would be an extreme example. Thus, there is much more to corporal punishment than bodily pain. While we may think of it as a crude retribution, it would be a mistake to assume that it is a straightforward one.

THE TRAUMA OF BEING PUNISHED IN PUBLIC

Both in ancient Rome and in early-modern Europe, there was a clear public-shaming component to punishment, which deepened the trauma of the prisoner and made an example of him or her in the sight of others. It

Left: The symbolism of water as a cleansing shower, combined with the shockingly palpable pain of a finely directed jet, meant that this Japanese punishment of the early 20th century was considered especially effective.

A good turnout around the pillory at London's Charing Cross in the 18th century, as recorded by the contemporary cartoonist Thomas Rowlandson. He, like many others of his time, felt that the pillory was in danger of turning justice into a degrading entertainment.

In England at that time, public punishments and executions had become a "day out" for many people, with stalls and entertainers setting up on the periphery; instead of inspiring fear, the punishments had become a source of ghoulish mirth and merriment.

A man is punished for his religious beliefs in 17th-century England. Flogging is not only a painful punishment but a demeaning one as well: modern criminologists question whether it deters offenders or—by assaulting their self-esteem—merely makes them even more likely to break the law again.

also had the effect of involving ordinary citizens in the punishment process, giving them the sense that they had a stake in their society—an important, if often unacknowledged, aspect of any justice system.

To some extent, this is still true today in cases where the entire nation may be brought together in its response to some celebrated murder trial. In part, of course, our interest is driven by curiosity, but our outrage at a crime also seems to offer us a means of social "bonding." This instinct is not

UNDER THE LASH

The most frequently used instrument of corporal punishment—in the Western tradition at any rate—has been the whip in its various cruel forms. The main variants employed throughout history were all used in ancient Rome, which had different whips for different degrees of punishment. First, there was the ferula, a flat piece of stiffened leather used to punish minor misdemeanors: generations of British schoolboys were strapped with something similar for not knowing their Latin verbs. It was a mild-enough punishment in its way, especially when compared to the scutica, whose lashing thongs were made of stiff parchment. Far worse, however, was the flagellum, or scourge,

whose ox-hide lashes were knotted at the ends to intensify the pain—or even weighted with sharp bone-splinters, metal balls, hooks, or spikes. It was by no means unheard of for slaves to die under the flagellum. In fact, if the poet Horace is to be believed, the executioner himself might collapse, exhausted, in the course of administering one of the marathon whippings so often ordered by the Roman courts.

strictly rational, of course, and it is by no means necessarily benign: the frenzy of the lynch mob is still remembered in the Southern states. Yet, whether we approve or not, this impulse has been present in every society and, when kept firmly in its place by official safeguards, surely has its part to play.

Having said this, however, we would hardly wish to return to a situation in which, as happened in England as late as the 17th century, a criminal was flogged in an open court—or whipped "at the cart's tail" through a city's streets. If such spectacles helped build community spirit, they did so at a fearful cost, being as degrading for the watchers as they were undignified for the victims. Yet the instinct to regard corporal punishment as a method of what a modern sporting coach or management consultant would call "team-building" survived until comparatively recently, especially in Europe. The British naval tradition of "flogging round the fleet" involved a wrongdoer being rowed from ship to ship (in an increasingly weakened and

This 19th-century engraving shows some of the hideous contraptions used to restrain insubordinate slaves in the American South: "medieval" devices like these lingered on well into the 19th century on some plantations.

traumatized state) until he had been whipped before the assembled crew of every naval vessel then in port.

"IF THY HAND OFFEND THEE..."

"Wherefore if thy hand or thy foot offend thee, cut them off, and cast them from thee: it is better for thee to enter into life halt or maimed, rather than having two hands or two feet to be cast into everlasting fire." The famous passage from St. Matthew's Gospel (18:8) recalls the uncompromising Old Testament demand for a punishment of precise physical equivalence: "an eye for an eye, a tooth for a tooth." Yet both these rulings had been

RUNNING THE GAUNTLET

In the armies of Britain and Europe, soldiers who broke the rules often had to "run the gauntlet" of their comrades, making their

way between facing ranks striking out with the flats of their swords, sticks, musket butts, or simply with boots and fists. This punishment, too, in its brutal way, can clearly be seen as a way of boosting troop morale—it was not, after all, so different from the various vicious "initiation" rituals that the soldiers themselves practiced on new recruits.

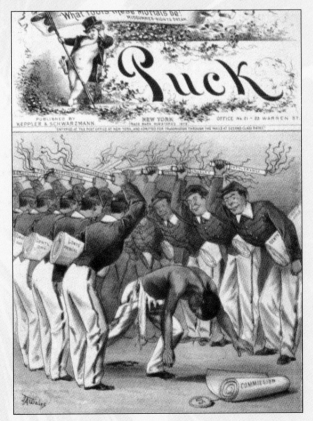

ANIMAL INDIGNITY

From the farms of the Roman Empire to the plantations of the Old South (see picture), the same sort of heavy stock whip was used for punishing wayward slaves as for driving cattle. This left the person doing the punishment in no doubt that his authority was in some sense "natural" and that the unfortunate person before him was somehow less than fully human.

This tradition of putting down victims by treating them like livestock endures today under some of the world's more repressive regimes, which use electrical cattle prods as instruments of punishment and torture for political prisoners.

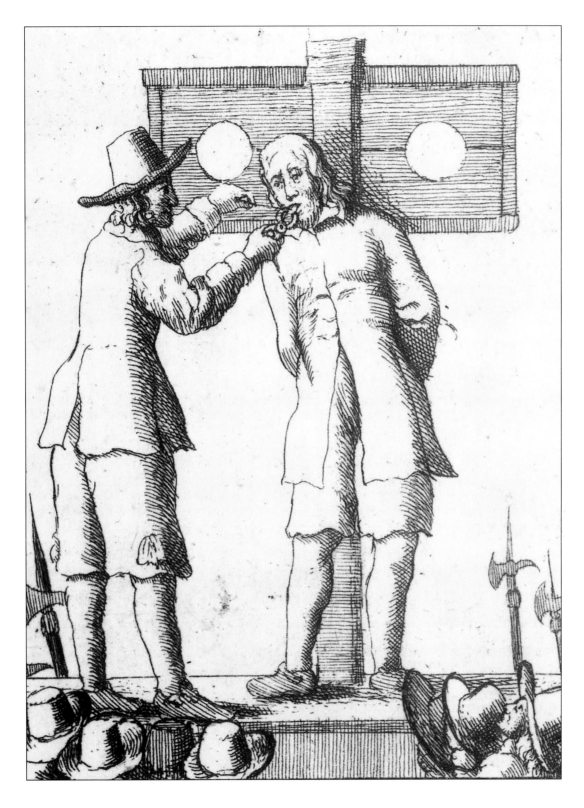

A cruel logic governs the punishment meted out to the Quaker James Naylor after his two hours in the London pillory, 1656: his tongue is pierced to prevent his ever repeating his scandalous religious doctrines.

anticipated—perhaps by as much as 1,000 years—by the ancient Indian text, the *Laws of Manu*. "He who sells for seed-corn that which is not seed-corn," Manu decreed; "he who takes up seed already sown, and he who destroys a boundary-mark, shall be punished by mutilation."

The idea that certain offenses should be recorded on the body seems to make sense at some deep level of human consciousness. In part, there seems to be some sort of symbolic logic involved. To the monks of the eighth century A.D., who were responsible for setting down the sanctions of church law in the *Byzantine Ecloga*, it seemed somehow appropriate that the sin of homosexuality be punished by castration, for example.

However, there was also a feeling that mutilation was needed to advertise an offense to society as a whole, so that people might be made aware of the authority of the law (and, from a more practical point of view, be warned of the presence of criminals among them). A widespread punishment in medieval Europe and still current in such Islamic nations as Saudi Arabia, the amputation of a thief's hand can clearly be seen to function on both these levels.

Petty criminals in Britain were frequently branded with red-hot metal stamps (in Scotland, a key was often used). Sometimes, this was done discreetly on the hand, so that if the person offended again in the future, the court would be aware of his or her criminal record. In other cases, the mark was made high on the cheek where all could see: a painful punishment, this would also serve as a lifelong badge of shame.

There was, for a considerable time, what amounted to a language of pain and disfigurement. For example, as late as the 18th century, English prostitutes might be punished with slits to the ears and nose—a direct attack on the physical attractiveness on which the women had traded. Similarly, blasphemers—those considered to have outraged God in their speech (although they were often, in fact, no more than conscientious religious reformers)—might have their tongues cut or pierced to prevent them from persisting in their "dreadful sins."

In 19th-century Ethiopia, people who dared to raise their hands against the rule of King Menelik could expect to have them chopped off and hung around their necks as ghastly mementoes.

Capital Punishment

The state can take no graver responsibility upon itself than the deliberate taking of an individual's life: throughout history, however, governments have been prepared to assume that right—or that duty. For some crimes, it has been felt, no lesser punishment would do—although there has often been disagreement over which particular crimes fall into that category.

In much of modern Europe, the death penalty has fallen into disuse, and there are influential American thinkers who regard its continuance as outdated, even barbaric. Other commentators see capital punishment as the cornerstone of the entire justice system—without that ultimate punishment, how can the rule of law have credibility?

"Thou shalt not kill," God commanded Moses—but does that constitute a biblical ban on the death penalty, as some would say, or a command that the crime of murder be punished with the utmost force? America's current position is something of a compromise. Although the death penalty is indeed used, it is reserved for the most grievous crimes of murder, with exhaustive efforts made to avoid any possible injustices.

TAKING LIFE

Criminals in the Egypt of the pharaohs were impaled on sharpened stakes and left to die in the desert sun; similar practices prevailed throughout the ancient Middle East. Pegged to tree trunks or walls with spikes or nails, prisoners were effectively put on public display as they died. Crucifixion, which we tend to regard as a distinctively Roman punishment, seems to

Left: To us today, the sight of a gaunt gallows mars the view of a picturesquely old-fashioned American courthouse, yet the death penalty remains our ultimate guarantee of the rule of law.

Three witches hang on the gallows in Essex, England, in an illustration of 1589: the indiscriminate way in which innocent women were persecuted at this time has given rise to the modern word "witch-hunt."

have been derived from these earlier Eastern practices. The Empire adopted these methods from its subject peoples in the area. (Prior to this, the Romans executed offenders in other ways, the most notorious of which was

DEATH BY FIRE

The Reformation of the 16 and 17th centuries was nothing less than a religious war, with Catholic monarchs administering fearful punishments in their attempt to stem the rising tide of what they saw as diabolical "heresy" (the holding of unorthodox views). Many thousands of faithful Catholics, meanwhile, were executed in the newly Protestant countries, as the authorities there sought to strengthen their shaky power.

History has perhaps been unfair in singling out the Spanish Inquisition as uniquely cruel, yet its proceedings do stand out in their terrible grandeur. The auto de fe ("act of faith"), the public ceremony at which heretics were first arraigned and then solemnly burned at the stake, was deliberately designed as a ritual enactment of the Last Judgment, complete with hellfire.

the throwing of traitors from the top of a cliff outside the city, the Tarpeian Rock.) The Gospel accounts of Jesus Christ's crucifixion constitute by far the most detailed account we have of the procedures involved—there seems no reason to doubt their general accuracy.

In medieval Europe, the favored method of execution was generally that of hanging, whether from a convenient tree or a specially constructed **scaffold** or **gibbet**. A noose was placed round the prisoner's neck and he or she was "turned off" from the rungs of a ladder. The person might then dangle helplessly through agonizing minutes, even hours, if a friend or bystander did not do him or her the favor of grabbing the person's legs and pulling them sharply down to break his or her neck. By the 16th century, a quicker and more dignified death was afforded by the practice of beheading, although this was reserved for more-aristocratic offenders. Two of the cast-off queens of King Henry VIII of England, Anne Boleyn and Catherine Howard, were to meet this fate in 1536 and 1542, respectively. Sir Walter Raleigh was beheaded in 1618 after falling foul of James I.

DETERRENT OR STATE SAVAGERY?

Death is supposed to be the penalty in cases in which the death penalty is enforced, but there have been times in history when death must have come as a welcome end to a protracted and terrible torture. The practice of "hanging, drawing, and quartering," used in England as late as the 17th century, involved hanging the victim until he hovered at the brink of death, then taking him down and drawing him through the streets on a length of fencing. The word "drawing" in the punishment's title, however, refers to the drawing out of his entrails while still alive. A skillful executioner could extract the prisoner's intestines and roast them on a fire as his helpless victim looked on, horrified. Only then would he be permitted to die, and his body cut up into quarters to be displayed on spikes in different cities of the kingdom. This threefold death was deemed appropriate for the threefold crime of treason against the king—an offense against the king

Those who fell foul of the religious conflicts of the 16th and 17th centuries could expect no Christian compassion from their enemies—Catholic or Protestant. Here, martyrs are drawn through streets lined with cheering, jeering crowds on their way to the gallows.

himself, against God his protector, and against his people.

Hangings were not always as appallingly spectacular as this. In fact, in some periods, they became almost routine. This was certainly the case in 18th century England under what was nicknamed—aptly enough—the "Bloody Code." It would be no exaggeration to say that English society in this period had become addicted to executions—and as with all addictions, the dosage constantly had to be stepped up to meet the growing need. By 1800, the list of offenses punishable by death had reached the

By the end of the 18th century, the London "hanging fair" had lost every last vestige of solemnity: the demand for something more dignified was becoming irresistible.

astounding—and absurd—figure of 200, covering crimes as minor as shoplifting or even stealing a sheep. Intended to serve as an example, public executions set the wrong sort of example altogether: a holiday spirit prevailed, as the mob turned out to cheer the condemned as heroes. Drink flowed, and laughter and ribaldry reigned. As novelist Henry Fielding (himself a local judge) pointed out, the general atmosphere of debauchery made a mockery of the idea that an execution could have deterrent value.

AN ENLIGHTENED AMERICA

The **depravity** of the English system was, in a sense, out of step with the times, since the 18th century had seen a revolution in attitudes across much of continental Europe. A new generation of scientists, artists, writers, and philosophers had helped build a new spirit of "Enlightenment," rejecting what they saw as the corruption, superstition, and barbarism of the

Thousands down the centuries have glimpsed eternity through the opening of the hangman's noose: how effective a deterrent it has been to others is hotly disputed.

In this late 19th-century engraving, two Russian revolutionaries go to their deaths in what were to prove the dying days of the czars themselves: however, their Communist successors would carry on killing where they had left off.

old traditions. The American republic was itself established on a wave of Enlightenment idealism: the Founding Fathers were strongly influenced by the progressive thinkers of Europe. This had profound implications for its approach to law and order and how punishment was applied.

Some radicals saw capital punishment as an inhumane remnant from the medieval ages, but it was too deeply rooted in Western law for abolition to

With minutes to go before Karla Faye Tucker's execution for a brutal double murder, guards at Huntsville, Texas' Walls Unit take up their positions.

be achieved. The spectacle was brought to an end, however. Pennsylvania held executions in private beginning in 1843, and other states followed suit over the remainder of the 19th century. America was generally quick to introduce what were seen as **humanitarian** advances—the use of the "long drop" in hangings was one of the first and most important of these. Rather than being turned off to a death of slow strangulation, the prisoner fell through an abruptly opening trapdoor: pulled up short by the rope, his neck was broken and—if the executioner's calculations had been accurate—he died instantly.

DEPRIVING LIFE WITHOUT INFLICTING PAIN

The United States has taken considerable trouble to find the most humane technique possible for execution: the punishment is supposed to lie in the deprivation of life, not in the inflicting of pain. With individual states free to select their own ways of administering the death penalty (and in some cases offering a choice to the prisoner concerned), a range of different methods has been used.

Among those most commonly employed has been the firing squad, based on the widely used military model, in which a row of men with rifles fires at a given signal. One will usually fire blank ammunition so that no squad member can feel sure he has been responsible for another person's death, because executions can take their psychological toll on the executioners. Similar safeguards are built into the other technologies used, with more than one executioner, for instance, throwing the switches for the electric chair. Since one switch will be "blind," each operator will have the consolation of feeling that he may not have been the one to make the fateful connection.

The most commonly used method of execution in America through much of the 20th century, the electric chair seemed like the last word in forward-looking humanity when it was introduced in 1890, although it never quite lived up to those early expectations. Hence, the introduction in

Essentially a military method of punishment, the firing squad is used more widely in countries under military rule: in this 1974 photograph, two armed robbers stand at the stake awaiting execution in Ilorin, Nigeria. Although the death penalty has been imposed intermittently in Nigeria, in 2002, a number of people were sentenced to death by stoning in the northern, predominantly Muslim, part of Nigeria under Islamic *sharia* law.

the 1920s of the gas chamber. Placed in an airtight space, the prisoner is killed by a poisonous cocktail of hydrochloric acid and potassium cyanide. The most modern method of all, the lethal injection, actually involves three injections administered in turn through an intravenous lead. The first (sodium thiopental) acts as a general anesthetic; the second (pancuronium bromide or pavulon) relaxes the muscles so completely that breathing stops; the third (potassium chloride) finishes the job by stopping the heart. This is the nearest we have yet come to finding a foolproof method of administering a quick and painless execution, although as anti-capital punishment campaigners have been quick to point out, it still falls short. In the first place, it can be extraordinarily difficult to find a suitable vein, meaning disturbing delays for the victim. Sometimes, too, a violent and distressing reaction to the drugs involved may be experienced.

A MOUNTING CONTROVERSY

However conscientiously it has tried to find the most humane ways of delivering the death penalty, America has found itself increasingly isolated in recent decades in its use of capital punishment. Most of the European countries (along with their former colonial possessions in the Third World) abandoned the practice altogether in the course of the 20th century. Today, the United States finds itself in some strange international company—with Communist China and North Korea, for example, as well as such Islamic fundamentalist states as Iran and Saudi Arabia.

Despite that, defenders say, the policy has proved its worth, and an elaborate system of checks and balances is in place to prevent abuses. Far from the sort of summary justice to be found in those other states, the death penalty in America is rigorously controlled, those condemned having access to an extensive range of appeals procedures at both a state and federal level. Those executed in America have spent an average of eight years on "Death Row": snap judgments are never made in what is, quite literally, a matter of life and death.

Today, it seems shadowy and sinister, and has largely been superceded by the gas chamber and lethal injection, but the electric chair was regarded as revolutionary when it was first introduced to American prisons in 1890.

The Rise of Rehabilitation

There may be more painful punishments than imprisonment—and more drastic ones, including that of death—but there is none that goes deeper to the heart of what it is to be human. The deprivation of an individual's physical liberty is a difficult one to withstand, no matter how comfortable the situation may be materially.

Often, of course, prisoners have been kept in appalling physical conditions: such confinement can be seen as a form of torture. Their captors have been unmoved, however. Prisons are not supposed to be palaces, they say, and are their inmates not there specifically for the sake of punishment? In the West in modern times, the feeling has grown that the punishment of crime is not in itself enough, that some attempt should also be made to reform the criminal. In an ideal world, this would involve his or her literal "re-formation" as a better person, but this has generally proved to be more easily said than done. The negative influence of other inmates, lack of resources, inadequate facilities—and above all, the stubbornness of human nature—may all marshal against any deep or meaningful changes in an individual prisoner. The effort has to go on, however. Prison officers learn to take encouragement from little triumphs, from every prisoner who succeeds in escaping the all-too-often endless cycle of release, re-offending, and re-imprisonment.

Left: Jonathan Wild, London's notorious "thieftaker general" turned gangleader, was consigned to Newgate to reflect on his crimes, but men like him could easily run their own criminal empires from inside prison.

Caged like an animal, the prisoner behind bars has the opportunity to consider how far he or she may have fallen short of the human decencies: the inmate who can learn that lesson may make a real contribution to society upon his or her release.

BEHIND BARS

The practice of imprisoning wrongdoers is almost certainly as old as civilization, and mere confinement has seldom seemed discouraging enough in itself as far as rulers have been concerned. From the Lion's Den into which the prophet Daniel was cast in the Bible to the rat-infested "Pit" in London's medieval Tower, the authorities did their best to ensure their prisoners' discomfort.

In truth, the sort of "offenders" imprisoned in ancient and medieval times—as indeed in many countries of the world today—were often those who had literally offended those individuals who were in power. Kings were quick to anger; high priests all-too-ready to see a slight—those who have to deal with dictators today are familiar with the difficulties. Most were, in other words, what we would think of as "political prisoners." The idea that there should be public prisons for those who had offended against society at large—robbers, thieves, con artists, murderers, and so on—emerged only gradually in early modern Europe.

The prisoners in this Hobart, Tasmania, chain gang were doubly punished: transported from an English home and then set to hard labor—yet what finally reformed them may have been the opportunities afforded by life in Australia.

REFORMING WOMEN

Members of an outspoken religious sect outraging "respectable" society with their beliefs, the Quakers came to know the prisons of England and America well from within. Conditions for women were particularly shocking, they found—and it was among Quaker women that the prison-reform movement eventually grew. The great pioneer was England's Elizabeth Fry (1780–1845, pictured) who, shocked by the conditions she found in London's Newgate Prison, started organizing prayer meetings—and even a self-help school—among the women there. A well-born and well-connected woman, she was able to take her arguments to the heart of the British political establishment, bringing a previously

hidden problem to public attention.

America's Abby Hopper Gibbons (1801–1893) also came from a Quaker background. She campaigned all her life for separate provisions to be made in prisons for female inmates. She also set up what we would call a halfway house to help ease women freed from prison back into the community, so that they—and their children—would have the best possible chance.

Rioting in 1780 under the anti-Catholic slogan of "No Popery," the London mob burned down Newgate Prison—a symbol for them not of legitimate law and order, but state oppression.

London's Newgate Prison was a byword for violence and squalor. Built to house 150 prisoners, Newgate usually contained up to 250 criminals—plus their families (and even pets). With drink freely available and gambling and violence everywhere, Newgate was, of course, no place for women or children. Yet where else were they to go once the family breadwinner was inside? With no protection or privacy in a place overcrowded with criminal men, physical and sexual abuse were inevitable.

Furthermore, the authorities supplied meager rations, so prisoners had to pay **extortionate** amounts for fresh food, and even bedding, from jailers who exploited their labor as a lucrative racket. Also on the take were the gangs that flourished inside, levying a semiofficial tax on new arrivals. There was every incentive for the strong to prey on the weak, for convicted prostitutes to continue to earn money by plying their trade, and for those who had entered in innocence to be thoroughly corrupted. In short, Newgate was far more likely to deprave and brutalize than to reform its unfortunate inmates.

FROM PRISON TO PENITENTIARY

The feeling that, far from improving their inmates, prisons were merely completing their corruption gained ground steadily in the course of the 18th century. Reformers, many of them Quakers, started imagining a new kind of prison, designed to bring about true "penitence," sorrow and repentance in its inmates. The first "**penitentiary**" was accordingly opened in America in 1829, in Philadelphia, in the predominantly Quaker state of Pennsylvania.

The traditional prison had stirred all its inmates into a squalid stew—the male and female, the old and young, the violent and the victim were all mixed up together in overcrowded and unsanitary conditions. In the penitentiary, in contrast, isolation was the key, the prisoner kept alone in a basic but adequate single cell. Stripped not only of corrupting company, but also of the normal trappings of identity, upon arrival inside, each inmate was given a uniform and a number to replace his name. In solitary confinement, it was thought, the prisoner could think about the sins he or she had committed.

The physical conditions in the old prisons had been an insult to civilization, with unsupervised overcrowding creating the conditions for appalling abuses. The new penitentiary addressed these challenges with great success, but as skeptical observers were soon pointing out, they

South Cell House
Penitentiary.
Menard Ill.
#4.

Straight lines for those who had strayed, from the stripes on their uniforms to the regimented rows of cells: the penitentiary at Menard, Illinois, around 1900, was preeminently a place of discipline and order.

"Picking oakum," separating out old ropes to obtain the raw fibers, was a characteristic occupation of convicts in 19th-century prisons: they spent many hours daily on such mind-numbing and fingertip-shredding work.

brought with them a new set of problems. The English novelist Charles Dickens, touring the Philadelphia facility in 1842, was horrified, writing, "The system is rigid, strict, and hopeless, and I believe it to be cruel and wrong. I hold this slow and daily tampering with the mysteries of the brain to be immeasurably worse than any torture of the body."

THE WORK ETHIC

If isolated introspection did not do the trick, how about hard labor? As the 19th century wore on, attempts were made to put punishment to work. Yet this was often easier said than done. Most jobs that needed doing offered too much variety and stimulus—too much fun, in fact—to seem like punishment, or else required too much supervision from officers to be practicable in prison. Hence, the desperate toil of the treadmill: an elongated mill wheel driven round in slow revolutions by the steps of

Members of a women's chain gang in Phoenix, Arizona, pick up litter on a city street: the idea is that they should make some amends to the community they have wronged.

prisoners—and all this energy was harnessed to make a fan on the prison roof go around and around.

Still more ingenious—but every bit as pointless—was the "crank," a stiff-handled machine that, turned painstakingly by the prisoner, sent a series of scoops rotating round a central wheel. At the bottom of their cycle, they collected sand from the bottom of the drum; arriving at the top, they duly dropped it again. The prisoner was expected to complete up to 10,000 complete revolutions in a working day, his total recorded by a meter on the machine.

Teams of convicts shackled together and set to carry out hard, physical labor on the country's highways, chain gangs often did much more genuinely useful work across America. This stripped men of their dignity, however, exposing prisoners to public humiliation. More imaginative attempts were made throughout the 20th century to make prisons part of the productive economy, with all sorts of industrial processes brought "inside." These have largely foundered on the profit-sapping realities of employment under prison conditions (the need for constant stoppages, searches, risk of sabotage, and so forth).

QUAKER REFORMERS AND REHABILITATION

The idea of **rehabilitation**—of equipping the individual for life on the right side of the law—dates back to the days of the first Quaker reformers. In recent decades, however, it has been interpreted in less narrowly moral terms: self-improvement is now seen as embracing education and the acquisition of skills for work and life. Many prisoners today take courses in everything from basic literacy to degree-level arts and sciences, often assisted in different ways by volunteers from the world outside. Prisoners who have skills and can support themselves through lawful work are much less likely to offend again.

These can be students giving basic instruction in reading and writing or world-famous musicians, from country singer Johnny Cash to rap star Rah

Popular country-and-western singer Johnny Cash has given many performances in prison: such visits may provide a vital boost in morale for inmates who are often badly in need of more self-esteem.

IN THE SPOTLIGHT

Inmates at California's San Quentin Prison were stunned when, in November 1957, members of the San Francisco Actors' Workshop staged a performance of Samuel Beckett's now-classic tragicomedy, *Waiting for Godot*, for their benefit. With its themes of existential bleakness and the endless wasting away of lonely lives, the play spoke directly to prisoners doing time.

Inspired, they decided to form their own San Quentin Drama Workshop, which made dramatic history in 1961 with a celebrated performance of Beckett's play. Since then, the company has won world renown for its interpretations of other works by the modernist master, its productions often directed by Beckett himself, before his death in 1989.

Digga. Such programs, all in their different ways, address the question of inmate self-esteem, which is today seen as crucial to successful integration into, and participation in, the wider community. At its best, this program provides a two-way process, with prisoners taken out to meet young people in schools and youth groups, fostering greater understanding and giving at-risk teenagers the benefits of their experiences.

Many of those who fall foul of the law turn out to have missed the full benefits of education for whatever reason: these young offenders at a prison in Swan Lake, Minnesota, have effectively gone back to school.

ESCAPE FROM PRISON

We have come a long way from the squalor of Newgate, but prison officials are well aware that, 300 years later, many of our problems remain the same. Prison gangs still oppress weaker, more vulnerable prisoners; the best-run penitentiaries are still "colleges of crime" in which first-time offenders acquire the attitudes and skills of career criminals. By taking the offender out of society, imprisonment risks jeopardizing the life and social skills a person has, although he or she may have been only insecurely anchored in their community to begin with.

Various attempts have been made in recent years to establish community-service programs in place of imprisonment: again, the aim is to foster a sense of self-worth and encourage the feeling of having an investment in society. The young criminal who has to meet his or her victim face-to-face and consider the consequences of his or her crime in personal terms may think harder before offending a second time. A recent innovation is **electronic tagging**, which is used for less-violent offenders and offers them the possibility of a halfway house, allowing close surveillance outside the damaging context of prison. This has obvious advantages in terms of prisoner morale (not to mention the enormous potential savings in public money), but unfortunately it has up to now been dogged by technological problems.

THE FUTURE

Our hunter-gatherer forebears seem to have lived without fear of crime or punishment. And while they seem enviable in that respect, we know that they also went without just about everything else that, for members of more sophisticated societies—from Assyria to modern-day America—has made life worth living.

We have to recognize that it seems to be part of our social nature to offend against others and that the need will always exist for societies to punish misbehaving members, whatever form this punishment will take.

This man is wearing an electronic ankle monitor after being released on parole in Ohio. The tag lets the authorities monitor the parolee and make sure he does not break the conditions of his parole, as well as discourage him from committing further crimes for fear of easy detection.

MAD OR BAD?

One summer's evening in 2001, Andrea Yates drowned her five children one by one in the bathtub: her eldest son, who was seven, had to be chased and caught before he could be murdered in his turn. The Houston, Texas, mother never tried to deny her crime—yet her defense team claimed that she was too mentally disturbed to be in any real sense morally responsible for her terrible actions.

The armed robber who kills the storekeeper who might identify him; the cornered criminal who shoots down a cop; the mugger who uses his knife on a victim who fights back—all these are heinous crimes, their perpetrators clearly setting themselves far beyond the limits of what any society can accept—yet they are not beyond the realms of our comprehension. Wicked, yet nevertheless rational, such crimes seem to come into a different category than those often unbelievable atrocities committed by "psychos" or serial killers of one sort or another.

The notion that mental instability might justify a claim to diminished responsibility has been current since the 18th century—yet has still to be fully accepted in the public mind. The killer who makes a plea of insanity stick is seen as "getting away" with his or her crime—though he or she will almost certainly spend the rest of his or her life in a secure institution.

Police officers, prosecutors, and judges dislike the idea that the law should have to give way to the expert opinion of the psychiatrist. Hence the paradoxical spectacle we sometimes see of prosecuting attorneys attempting to affirm the fundamental sanity of men and women who are acknowledged to have committed the most bizarrely outrageous murders.

Reformers' hopes that "progress" might be made, that humankind might ultimately prove to be "perfectible" have, for the most part, been disappointed: our deeper nature has resisted attempts at improvement, however humane.

Not that those who support punishment have anything to triumph about: its results have been equally dismal. However harsh the penalties, we have never managed to frighten the hardened criminal into compliance. If neither kindness nor cruelty works, what are we to do? Society demands we do something: if we cannot abolish crime, we may at least attempt to keep levels down; whatever our misgivings and whatever its shortcomings, punishment is here to stay.

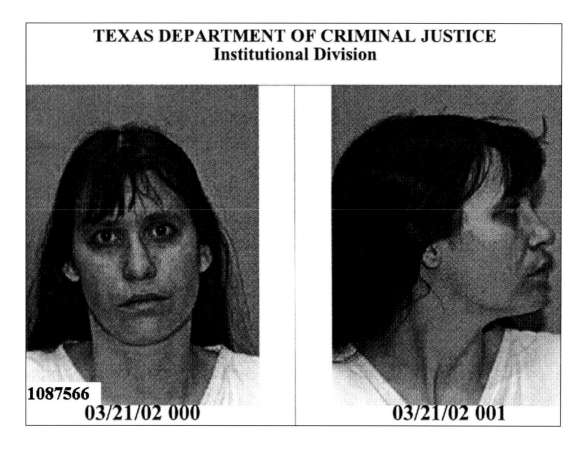

TEXAS DEPARTMENT OF CRIMINAL JUSTICE
Institutional Division

1087566
03/21/02 000

03/21/02 001

Andrea Yates, the convicted child killer, is pictured in this Texas Department of Criminal Justice photo shot in Gatesville, Texas. Found guilty in 2002 of drowning her five children while she was deeply psychotic, Yates was taken to a prison in eastern Texas. She began a life sentence that justice officials estimate will keep her behind bars for a minimum of 40 years.

GLOSSARY

Adultery: voluntary sexual relations between a married person and someone who is not his or her spouse

Atheism: a belief that there is no God or gods

Covetousness: having a craving for possession

Creed: a set of fundamental beliefs

Depravity: moral corruption, or an instance of this

Electronic tagging: this involves attaching an electronic device to a criminal after he or she has been released, in order to track the person to ensure that he or she does not commit a crime again

Ethics: the discipline dealing with what is good and bad and with moral duty and obligation

Extortionate: grossly excessive

Gibbet: an upright post with a projecting arm for hanging the bodies of executed criminals as a warning

Humanitarian: promoting the interests and welfare of humanity

Karma: concept found in Indian religions, including Hinduism and Buddhism, by which a person's conduct in one life will have bearing on his or her status in another existence

Kosher: sanctioned by Jewish law

Penitentiary: type of prison developed in the 19th century with the intention not just of punishing, but also of promoting "penitence"—regret for wrongs committed

Piety: devoutness

Pillory: a device formerly used for publicly punishing offenders consisting of a wooden frame with holes in which the head and hands can be locked

Rehabilitation: literally, "restoring the ability": reequipping an individual for life in society

Scaffold: a platform where a criminal is executed

Secular: having nothing to do with religion

Totem: an object, in particular an animal, symbolizing a clan or individual, and often having ritual associations

Terefah: a foodstuff forbidden by Jewish dietary laws

CHRONOLOGY

1775 B.C.:	Babylonian "Code of Hammurabi": the first known legal system is recorded in script; pharaonic Egypt is punishing enemies by impalement.
800:	Early Romans throw traitors to their deaths from the Tarpeian Rock.
500:	Idea of an afterlife is gaining ground in Jewish thought.
480:	Birth of Gautama Buddha in what is now Tilaurakot, modern Nepal; as a young man, he travels in India, which is where he establishes the religion that bears his name.
450:	Roman law is written down officially in "Twelve Tables."
300–100:	*Manusmrti*, "Laws of Manu," are written down by India's Hindu scholars.
100:	With their empire expanding into the Middle East, the Romans are influenced by local practices—like crucifixion.
A.D.	Birth of Christ; introduction of gospel of forgiveness.
535:	Complete codification of Roman law is undertaken on the orders of the Emperor Justinian.
c. 1000:	Hanging is well established in Europe as the main method of execution; "hanging, drawing, and quartering" for traitors is continued well into the 17th century.
1530:	German religious reformer Martin Luther makes his decisive break with Rome, initiating what is known as the "Reformation"; thousands are put to death by both sides in the century or so of religious conflict that follows.
1700–1800:	Under the "Bloody Code," the number of offenses punishable by death in England rises to 200; supposedly solemn public executions become raucous "hanging fairs."
1829:	First "penitentiary" opens in Philadelphia, Pennsylvania; despite drawbacks, the example is widely copied in both America and Europe.
1834:	Pennsylvania moves executions inside correctional facilities.

1890: William Kemmler is the first person to die in the electric chair.

1924: First use of cyanide gas in executions by the state of Nevada.

1961: San Quentin Drama Workshop stages acclaimed performance of Samuel Beckett's play, *Waiting for Godot*—just one sign of a new emphasis being placed on prisoners' personal development.

1972: *Furman v. Georgia* Supreme Court ruling deems capital punishment "cruel and unusual punishment"—and therefore unconstitutional; capital punishment, to all intents and purposes, is abolished in the United States.

1976: *Gregg v. Georgia* ruling effectively overturns *Furman v. Georgia* decision.

1977: National Crime Prevention Council (NCPC) is established.

1994: Washington, D.C. introduces new "Three Strikes And You're Out" legislation, meaning long prison sentences for persistent (even if minor) criminals; other states quickly follow suit.

FURTHER INFORMATION

Useful Web Sites

www.ojp.usdoj.gov/bjs: The Department of Justice's Web site has up-to-the-minute data on crime and punishment in contemporary America.

www.asphistory.com: This provides a history of Anamosa State Penitentiary, Iowa.

www.helsinki.fi/~tuschano/cp/: This provides a wide international perspective on the death penalty.

Further Reading

Farrington, Karen. *A History of Punishment and Torture*. New York: Hamlyn, 2000. This book provides a survey of the sometimes cruel ways in which societies have maintained discipline down the ages.

Friedman, Lawrence Meir. *Crime and Punishment in American History*. New York: Basic Books, 1994. This book examines the American experience of punishment in close-up, from colonial times onward.

Johnson, Robert. *Death Work: A Study of the Modern Execution Process*. Belmont, CA: Wadsworth, 1997. This book looks at how capital punishment works in practice in the present day.

Kerrigan, Michael. *The Instruments of Torture*. New York: Lyons Press, 2001.

Morris, Norval and David J. Rothman. *The Oxford History of the Prison: The Practice of Punishment in Western Society*. New York: Oxford University Press, 1997. This book provides an in-depth portrait of punishment in Western society.

Palmer, Louis J. *Encyclopedia of Capital Punishment in the United States.* Jefferson, NC: McFarland & Company, 2002. This weighty volume provides an overview of the subject.

About the Author

Michael Kerrigan was born in Liverpool, England, and educated at St. Edward's College, from where he won an Open Scholarship to University College, Oxford. He lived for a time in the United States, spending time first at Princeton, followed by a period working in publishing in New York. Since then, he has been a freelance writer and journalist, with commissions across a wide range of subjects, but with a special interest in social policy and defense issues. Within this field, he has written on every region of the world.

His work has been published by leading international educational publishers, including the BBC, Dorling Kindersley, Time-Life, and Reader's Digest Books. His work as a journalist includes regular contributions to the *Times Literary Supplement*, London, as well as a weekly column in the *Scotsman* newspaper, Edinburgh, where he now lives with his wife and their two small children.

INDEX